GOLIATH

Born For The Moment

VANCE K. JACKSON, JR.

Goliath: Born For The Moment
A 21-Day Leadership Devotional
ISBN: 978-1-7369832-3-2
Published by 5th Gen Publishing, LLC.
© 2021 Vance K. Jackson, Jr.
www.VanceKJackson.com

Printed in the United States of America. All rights reserved. No portion of this book may be reproduced, stored in a retrieval system, or transmitted in any form or by any means—electronic, mechanical, photocopy, recording, scanning, or other—except for brief quotations in critical reviews or articles, without the prior written permission of the publisher.

Scripture quotations taken from the Amplified® Bible (AMPC), Copyright © 1954, 1958, 1962, 1964, 1965, 1987 by The Lockman Foundation Used by permission. www.lockman.org

Scripture quotations from The Authorized King James Version (KJV). Rights in the Authorized Version in the United Kingdom are vested in the Crown. Reproduced by permission of the Crown's patentee, Cambridge University Press.

Scripture quotations marked (MSG) are taken from THE MESSAGE, copyright © 1993, 2002, 2018 by Eugene H. Peterson. Used by permission of NavPress, represented by Tyndale House Publishers. All rights reserved.

Scripture quotations marked (NIV) are taken from the Holy Bible, New International Version®, NIV®. Copyright © 1973, 1978, 1984, 2011 by Biblica, Inc.™ Used by permission of Zondervan. All rights reserved worldwide. www.zondervan.com The "NIV" and "New International Version" are trademarks registered in the United States Patent and Trademark Office by Biblica, Inc.™

Scripture quotations marked (NLT) are taken from the Holy Bible, New Living Translation, copyright © 1996, 2004, 2015 by Tyndale House Foundation. Used by permission of Tyndale House Publishers, Inc., Carol Stream, Illinois 60188. All rights reserved.

Library of Congress Cataloging-in-Publication Data
Library of Congress Control Number: 2021912971

TABLE OF CONTENTS

DAY 1
Born for the Moment 9

DAY 2
Don't Waste Your Moment 11

DAY 3
The Least Likely 13

DAY 4
Born To Lead 17

DAY 5
Preparation for the Throne 19

DAY 6
Your Anonymity Has Purpose. 21

DAY 7
The Uncircumcised Philistine .25

DAY 8
Emotional Intelligence: Kings Keep Their Composure 29

DAY 9
Mental Tenacity: Kings Kill Problems. 33

DAY 10
God Looks on the Heart. 37

DAY 11
A King in Sheep's Clothing. 41

DAY 12
The Head of Goliath 43

DAY 13
Kings Are Born in Crisis. 47

DAY 14
Don't Covet the Crown.............................49

DAY 15
After the Kill.....................................53

DAY 16
A Nation Governed by Fear........................57

DAY 17
Don't Grow Bitter.................................59

DAY 18
Draw Nigh To God.................................61

DAY 19
Can God Trust You?...............................63

DAY 20
No Fear. It's Time to Pursue......................65

DAY 21
Declaration over Fear.............................67

Day 1

BORN FOR THE MOMENT

And David spake to the men that stood by him, saying, What shall be done to the man that killeth this Philistine, and taketh away the reproach from Israel? for who is this uncircumcised Philistine, that he should defy the armies of the living God?

1 SAMUEL 17:26 KJV

In the middle of a national crisis, David declared, "Who is this uncircumcised Philistine?" In a moment when Israel was paralyzed by fear, David presented a solution that would free the nation from the paralytic grip of the enemy. In a moment when uncertainty plagued Israel—God raised up David to lead the nation out of its "Purpose Paralysis."

What has your God-given purpose bound? Your gifts, wisdom, experience, and insight weren't meant to stay dormant. You weren't meant to stay hidden. God has given you skills, gifts, talents, and abilities that were meant to lead and inspire generations. God has planted gifts inside of you that were meant to be used to set others free.

Let God use you. Let God lead you to set others free. Free from the tyranny of fear. Free from every stronghold. Free from the paralytic grip of the enemy. It's time to pour out everything that God has poured into you.

You were built to create. You were created to innovate. You were molded by God to solve problems that others cannot solve. God created your hands to war against the kingdom of darkness and to execute against the power of the enemy. Use the gifts that God has given you to diligently execute in your God-given purpose and take back everything that the enemy has stolen.

Deploy the gifts that God has invested inside of you. Unveil, to the world, what God has called you to do. Start that business. Launch that ministry. Write that book. Go back to school. Execute upon that idea. Whatever the idea, whatever the assignment, no matter the mandate—it's time to execute.

What has God called you to do? What problem(s) were you called to solve? What calamities were you called to calm? What God-given gifts, talents, and abilities has God given you to deploy as weapons to crush and conquer Goliath?

You were called to lead. You were born to calm crisis. You were born to bring peace. You were created to bring order to chaos. You were created, by God, to conquer new territories. You were born to crush and kill Goliath and to take back everything that the enemy has held hostage.

You weren't born by accident. You are not an afterthought. You are not an accident. You were intentionally crafted, created, and molded by God to impact the world. You were created to impact this generation. You were born for the moment. You were born for such a time as this.

Day 2

DON'T WASTE YOUR MOMENT

You were created, by God, for this very moment. This is your moment. This is your time. This is your season. Don't miss your moment. This is your hour. Just like David, who had a series of private catalytic moments in the field, David did not waste his moment. When it was time for David to lead, he executed, and he lifted the burden and removed the reproach from off of Israel.

David's private catalytic moments gave him momentum to crush and kill Goliath. David's private moments were critical for his future success. David was born to stand up in the face of national adversity and calamity. David was born to protect, lead, and transform a generation. David was called to kill Goliath. David was called to solve Israel's "Goliath Dilemma." What problem(s) are you called to solve?

No matter how seemingly minor your private moments are—every moment has purpose. Moments carry weight. Moments have significance. Moments have power. Moments have value. Moments carry momentum, and they shape the trajectory of your destiny. Make your moment count. Don't waste the moment.

David served God in private. David obeyed God in private. David submitted to God and he protected his father's flock in private. It was in these private moments, when no one was watching, where David's character was groomed, shaped, and cultivated. It was in these private moments of obedience and submission where David was cultivated by God to kill giants and prepared him to lead nations.

Leadership starts in private. It is your private preparation that propels you to reign on public platforms. Your private moments matter and they prepare you to conquer public platforms. Don't despise your private preparation. Don't despise your small beginnings. Don't minimize your private victories. Your private moments matter.

What is God preparing you for in private? What giant is God preparing you to slay? What strategic problem is God preparing you to solve? It's time to kill what has been plaguing your family for generations. It's time to crush what's been taunting over your career. It's time to kill what's been taunting over your business. It's time to crush what's been weighing you down. It's time to kill the Giant. It's time to kill Goliath. Kill the problem. Seize your moment. This is your moment. Now is the time.

Day 3

THE LEAST LIKELY

According to 1 Samuel 17:17-18 KJV, David was sent on an assignment by his father, Jesse, to deliver food to his brothers. Jesse had sent David on a simple errand. Jesse had no clue that his son, David, would come back with the head of Goliath in his hand.

1 Samuel 17:17–18 KJV declares, "And Jesse said unto David his son, Take now for thy brethren an ephah of this parched corn, and these ten loaves, and run to the camp to thy brethren; And carry these ten cheeses unto the captain of their thousand, and look how thy brethren fare, and take their pledge."

Notice in 1 Samuel 17:17–18 KJV, David did not wake up thinking that he was going to slay a giant. In fact, killing a giant was probably the last thing on David's mind. Think about this for a moment. Jesse had sent his son away with cheese and bread in order to feed and serve others—but David came back, leading the army of Israel. David came back with the head of Goliath in his hand. What a remarkable feat!

More often than not, it is the least likely, and the overlooked, who God raises up to lead nations. It is hidden kings, like David, who God raises up to deliver His people out of bondage. It is the least likely, and the overlooked, those who are working behind the scenes—God brings them out of the shadows and on to global stages. Let God prepare you in private. Get ready. Stay ready. God is raising up a generation who will come back with the head of Goliath.

David's private preparation and consecration positioned him to kill what others could not slay. Consecrate yourself in private. Serve in private and let God reward you openly.

Although God was privately preparing David for kingship—David served and honored his father faithfully while he was in the field. In fact, this is one of the many leadership principles that we can learn from David. Although David was born to lead nations and kill giants, David faithfully served in the field. Yes, you were born to lead industries and to take on "Goliath-sized problems"—you were also born to selflessly serve others. Leadership is born out of selfless service.

In 1 Samuel 16:12–13 KJV, Samuel had anointed David in front of Jesse and his brethren. Although David was anointed by Samuel, in the midst of his brethren and his father to be Israel's next king, his father still kept him serving in the field—tending to his sheep. Even though David was anointed as king, David didn't allow his lack of recognition from his family to deter his private preparation. Don't get bitter in the wilderness. Stay focused and keep executing behind the scenes.

David was anointed by Samuel as the next king of Israel and yet his father still sent him on "cheese errands." Even during national calamity, his brothers still did not see David as the solution, but rather they saw David as a boy tending sheep in the wilderness. 1 Samuel 17:28 KJV expounds on this point further, "And Eliab his eldest brother heard when he spake unto the men; and Eliab's anger was kindled against David, and he said, Why camest thou down hither? and with whom hast thou left those few sheep in the wilderness? I know thy pride, and the naughtiness of thine heart; for thou art come down that thou mightest see the battle."

Don't allow the negative opinion of others to rule over your heart. Don't allow their perception of you to weigh you down. If David had been emotionally crushed by the opinions of his brothers—he would not have had the courage to crush Goliath. Don't fold under the weight of man's opinion.

If David had folded under the weight of Eliab's opinion or even waited for his father's approval, David would not have fully walked out his destiny and killed Goliath. David did not allow man's opinion to taint his heart. Don't allow the opinion of man and their perception of you to cause you to back down from pursuing your purpose. Don't let your gifts, talents, and abilities die under the weight of the approval or disapproval of others. Don't back down. Don't become bitter. Don't shrink. Don't fold. Choose to be bold. Choose to obey God.

Don't allow bitterness to harden your heart. Don't allow bitterness to distract you from fulfilling your purpose. Don't get bitter during your preparation. Don't allow bitterness to derail you. Don't allow bitterness to stunt your spiritual development. Don't allow bitterness to paralyze your emotional development. Bitterness will isolate you and stunt your "gift development."

If David was more focused on bowing to the opinions of man—then he would not have been ready to function as king or operate on the global platform that God had prepared for him. Preparation is a choice. Preparation requires discipline. Kings are cultivated behind the scenes. Kings are developed when no one is watching. God creates kings in obscurity. God prepares kings in the field.

Kings aren't built overnight. God led David while he was in the field. God showed David what to do next while he was in the field. While you're in the field, ask God to order your steps. Ask God to lead your next steps.

God sharpened David while he was in the field. David was strengthened by God in the field. David was taught by God while he was in the field. David was led by God in the field. David was counseled by God in the field.

Although David was isolated by his family in the field—God was with him every step of the way. God never left David. God never abandoned him. In fact, David developed a stronger relationship with God while he was in the field. Don't despise the background. Don't despise the field. The field is preparation for your purpose. The field is preparation for your call.

Day 4

BORN TO LEAD

While David was in the field, tending to his father's sheep, God groomed David. While David was in the background, overseeing sheep and goats, God had David's ear. God groomed David while he was in the wilderness. The field wasn't a means to punish David—the field was meant to prepare David for his future.

David's isolation wasn't a prison sentence—it was a means to develop intimacy. The future has a language and it takes intimacy and diligence to prepare for it. God is intimately preparing you for your future. God was sharpening David while he was in the field. God groomed David while he was in the background. God led David while he was in the field. The wilderness wasn't punishment—the wilderness was only for a season.

It was in these private moments where God cultivated David as a leader. God cultivated David while he was in the wilderness. It was in these intimate moments where David's execution and precision were birthed. God showed David how to execute, lead, and how to solve problems while he was in the field. It was in these private and intimate "field moments" where God showed David how to steward and protect the platform that was under his care.

Before David had a global stage, before David led armies, David obeyed God in the field. When no one was watching, David put his life on the line for his sheep. Before David was elevated, God was with him. Before David was promoted, God was with him. Before David stood before kings, God was with him. Before David was crowned as king, God was with him. Let God lead you and show you how to solve problems in private. Before God gives you global stages, let God intimately lead the work of your hands.

While you're in the background, let God sharpen you when no one is watching. Let God show you how to execute, produce, and perform when no one is watching. Ask God to give you wisdom to execute in private. James 1:5 NLT declares, "If you need wisdom, ask our generous God, and he will give it to you. He will not rebuke you for asking."

Ask God to give you the wisdom to solve problems on the platform that He's given you. Ask God to show you how to solve problems on your job. Ask God to show you how to solve problems in your family. Ask God to show you how to solve problems in your business. Ask God to show you how to solve problems in your community. Ask God to show you how to solve problems in your ministry.

No matter the circumstance—no matter the platform—ask God to give you wisdom on how to solve problems. Be a "Problem Solver" and steward your platform well. Don't despise your small beginnings—they were meant to prepare you.

Day 5

PREPARATION FOR THE THRONE

David solved smaller problems in the field before he graduated to killing Goliath. The lion and the bear were "practice"— and the field was preparation for the throne. David was not an overnight success—God prepared David while he was in the field. Your private preparation has purpose. Look at your private moments as opportunities to prepare for the future.

Your private preparation is not in vain. Diligent preparation propagates success. You may be gifted, you may be talented, you may be anointed; however, potential without diligent preparation and execution will lead to stagnation and frustration. You must prepare for success. You must prepare for the future.

Although David was anointed to be king, anointing alone was not enough to reign as king. In order to handle the weight and magnitude of the throne, God trained David while he was in the field. Diligence is learned in the field. Discipline is sharpened in the field. Character is developed in the field. Develop your character in private and let God give you public platforms. Let God prepare you in private. Don't let the weight of the wilderness crush you. Let God lead you in the wilderness. Discipline, diligence, and execution are required at the next level.

David could have allowed the lion and the bear to devour the sheep, but he decided to protect the platform and the sheep that were under his stewardship. Jesse entrusted David to oversee and steward the affairs of the field. David protected the sheep when no one was watching. David protected the platform when no one was looking.

Let God lead you in private. Let God shape and mature your character in private. Let God prepare you to kill giants. Don't let the magnitude of the moment crush you. Private preparation develops you for public platforms. Private diligence prepares you for public mantles. David was anointed in private, but he was born for public authority. God prepared David in private, but he was born to publicly kill giants.

What are you called to kill? What giants are you called to slay? Kill the giant and lead your family. Kill the giant and lead your community. Kill the giant and lead your city. Kill the giant and lead your nation. Kill the giant and lead nations. Kill the giant and lead this generation. You were born to kill giants. You were born to solve problems. You were born to crush and overcome obstacles. You were born to break generational cycles. The field has purpose—God is preparing you for the throne.

Day 6

YOUR ANONYMITY HAS PURPOSE

David's anonymity was one of his greatest assets and weapons against the enemy. David's anonymity had purpose. God used David's anonymity as a strategic weapon against the enemy. Let God use your anonymity as a strategic attack against Satan. Just because you're "hidden" does not mean that you're not on God's mind. Just because you're in the background does not mean that you're not at the forefront of God's heart.

God established David privately in order to prepare him for this very public moment. David's isolation was not a means of punishment. God used David's private moments as a means of catalytic preparation that would propel David to the next level. Sometimes God uses seemingly obscure seasons to shift your perspective. Sometimes God uses the wilderness to sharpen your development. Don't despise your small and private beginnings.

Notice what 1 Samuel 17:32–37 KJV declares, "And David said to Saul, Let no man's heart fail because of him; thy servant will go and fight with this Philistine. And Saul said to David, Thou art not able to go against this Philistine to fight with him: for thou art but a youth, and he a man of war from his youth. And David said unto Saul, Thy servant kept his father's sheep, and there came a lion, and a bear, and took a lamb out of the flock: And I went out after him, and smote him, and delivered it out of his mouth: and when he arose against me, I caught him by his beard, and smote him, and slew him. Thy servant slew both the lion and the bear: and this uncircumcised Philistine shall be as one of them, seeing he hath defied the armies of the living God. David said moreover, The Lord that delivered me out of the paw of the lion, and out of the paw of the bear, he will deliver me out of the hand of this Philistine. And Saul said unto David, Go, and the Lord be with thee."

Goliath was not familiar with David's private track record. David's private victories gave him the résumé and the track record that he needed to present to the king. David's private preparation set him apart from his peers and from those who were afraid to execute.

May your private preparation set you apart from your peers. May your private preparation give you the courage to execute. May your private victories propel you forward and give you the courage to kill giants. May your private diligence prepare you to stand before kings.

It's time to execute. It's time to propel forward. Choose to prepare in private and execute in public. Don't let fear hold you back from pursuing your purpose. Pursue and take back everything that the enemy has stolen. God has prepared you for this moment.

Execution without preparation will lead to destruction. David prepared and tested his weapons in private long before he stood before Goliath. David tested his arsenal in private. David tested his weapons in the wilderness. David knew his strengths and his weaknesses—he had mastered his battle strategies in private. David knew what tactics worked for him in private and he also discovered what strategies didn't work for him. Great leaders know their strengths, and they know their weaknesses.

Notice what David had declared in 1 Samuel 17:34–37 KJV, "And David said unto Saul, Thy servant kept his father's sheep, and there came a lion, and a bear, and took a lamb out of the flock: And I went out after him, and smote him, and delivered it out of his mouth: and when he arose against me, I caught him by his beard, and smote him, and slew him. Thy servant slew both the lion and the bear: and this uncircumcised Philistine shall be as one of them, seeing he hath defied the armies of the living God. David said moreover, The Lord that delivered me out of the paw of the lion, and out of the paw of the bear, he will deliver me out of the hand of this Philistine. And Saul said unto David, Go, and the Lord be with thee."

Kings give access to platforms. Kings give access to opportunity. May God grant you favor with kings. May God grant you access to those in authority. May God open doors of favor, opportunity, and influence.

Go and represent God in business, in ministry, in school, in the boardroom, and on your job. Go and solve the problems that others cannot solve. It's time to go, and do what God has called you to do.

Saul declared, "Go, and the Lord be with thee." Go, and the Lord be with thee. Go, and kill Goliath. David had the solution—kill Goliath. You have the solution—it's time to kill Goliath.

Day 7

THE UNCIRCUMCISED PHILISTINE

Notice what David had declared in 1 Samuel 17:26 KJV, "And David spake to the men that stood by him, saying, What shall be done to the man that killeth this Philistine, and taketh away the reproach from Israel? for who is this uncircumcised Philistine, that he should defy the armies of the living God?"

Notice David's word choice when referring to Israel's enemy. David calls Goliath an "Uncircumcised Philistine." The fact that David calls Goliath an "Uncircumcised Philistine" is critical to the battle that he's about to face. In fact, this peculiar naming convention, "Uncircumcised Philistine," reveals David's mental state and internal leadership framework as to how to lead in crisis. In fact, David killed Goliath, in his head, before he ever had a weapon in his hand.

The name "Uncircumcised Philistine," that David decides to use, teaches us several key leadership principles about spiritual warfare and leading in chaotic circumstances. The word "Uncircumcised" was introduced back in Genesis 17:10 KJV, where God instituted the act of circumcision to Abraham.

This act, "the circumcision," acknowledges the covenant that God made to Abraham and his seed. "This is my covenant, which ye shall keep, between me and you and thy seed after thee; Every man child among you shall be circumcised." Genesis 17:10 KJV.

The circumcision was an outward expression of an internal spiritual Covenant that was made between God and man.

According to Strong's Concordance, the Hebrew word for, "circumcise" is "muwl" (H4135), which means "to cut." This "cutting away of the flesh" signified that man had submitted his flesh and life to God. When one was circumcised, it was a symbol of the covenant that God had made with Abraham.

David declared in 1 Samuel 17:26 KJV, "And David spake to the men that stood by him, saying, What shall be done to the man that killeth this Philistine, and taketh away the reproach from Israel? for who is this uncircumcised Philistine, that he should defy the armies of the living God?"

David knew that this "Uncircumcised Philistine" was trespassing on God's ground and against God's people. David knew that this battle was not about man—but this battle was about the Covenant of God. God keeps His Covenant. God keeps His Word.

David identified that this was indeed a spiritual battle. David knew whose Covenant he was under. David knew that he served a bigger God. David knew that he had already won the battle against this "Uncircumcised Philistine" because his God was greater than the enemy that he faced. In fact, the battle was over before it began.

Notice the spiritual dynamic displayed here between the Israelites and the Philistines. 1 Samuel 17:3 KJV gives an account of the battle that was underway, "And the Philistines stood on a mountain on the one side, and Israel stood on a mountain on the other side: and there was a valley between them."

The Philistines were standing on one mountain and the Israelites were standing on another mountain. In fact, the Philistines were illegally invading on the Children of Israel's territory. So, when David declared the statement, "For who is this uncircumcised Philistine, that he should defy the armies of the living God?" David was declaring, "Who is this unprotected and uncircumcised enemy who has invaded our borders given to us by God?"

David understood that Israel's Covenant with God and the promise given to Israel was greater than Goliath's threat. Therefore, David understood that he was not operating and fighting in his own carnal strength. David was backed by a Stronger Authority. David was backed by a Stronger Covenant. David was backed by God.

When you are in Christ, choose to remember that your Covenant is greater than any enemy that you face. Your steps are ordered by God. Your destiny is backed by God. You are backed by God Himself. Pursue the giant and cut off his head.

Day 8

EMOTIONAL INTELLIGENCE: KINGS KEEP THEIR COMPOSURE

There are several key emotional leadership principles and leadership dynamics that we can extract from this single moment in Israel's history between David and Goliath. First, let's examine the emotional condition of the army of Israel during this time. Let's examine this heated encounter between the men of Israel and the Philistines outlined in 1 Samuel 17:1–11 KJV: "Now the Philistines gathered together their armies to battle, and were gathered together at Soco, which belongeth to Judah, and pitched between Soco and Azekah, in Ephes–dammim. And Saul and the men of Israel were gathered together, and pitched by the valley of Elah, and set the battle in array against the Philistines. And the Philistines stood on a mountain on the one side, and Israel stood on a mountain on the other side: and there was a valley between them. And there went out a champion out of the camp of the Philistines, named Goliath, of Gath, whose height was six cubits and a span. And he had an helmet of brass upon his head, and he was armed with a coat of mail; and the weight of the coat was five thousand shekels of brass. And he had greaves of brass upon his legs, and a target of brass between his shoulders. And the staff of his spear was like a weaver's beam;

and his spear's head weighed six hundred shekels of iron: and one bearing a shield went before him. And he stood and cried unto the armies of Israel, and said unto them, Why are ye come out to set your battle in array? am not I a Philistine, and ye servants to Saul? choose you a man for you, and let him come down to me. If he be able to fight with me, and to kill me, then will we be your servants: but if I prevail against him, and kill him, then shall ye be our servants, and serve us. And the Philistine said, I defy the armies of Israel this day; give me a man, that we may fight together. When Saul and all Israel heard those words of the Philistine, they were dismayed, and greatly afraid."

1 Samuel 17:11 KJV gives a clear depiction of the emotional state of Israel during this time. Notice, the entire army of Israel was paralyzed with fear. 1 Samuel 17:11 KJV declares, "When Saul and all Israel heard those words of the Philistine, they were dismayed, and greatly afraid."

1 Samuel 17:11 KJV also states that even king Saul was paralyzed with fear. Imagine the Army of Israel's response when their leader, King Saul, shriveled back when he saw Goliath. The emotional condition of the army was merely a manifestation of the heart of their leader. King Saul retreated—and his army followed suit.

Israel needed a leader who would stand up in times of crisis. This was not a time for Israel to stand down—it was a time to stand up. It was time to stand up in adversity. It was time to stand up when a crisis threatened to enslave Israel.

Goliath wanted to enslave Israel. According to Strong's Concordance, the name "Goliath" (H1555) means "Splendor." Goliath was indeed a weapon of the Philistine Army. In fact, according to 1 Samuel 17:4 KJV, Goliath was a "champion" who had a track record of defeating those who would contest him. Goliath was not only a "champion" with an impressive track record, but as his name signifies, his physical presence was indeed, "splendid."

According to 1 Samuel 17:4 KJV, the Bible declares that Goliath was six cubits and a span tall, "And there went out a champion out of the camp of the Philistines, named Goliath, of Gath, whose height was six cubits and a span." Which means he was more than nine feet tall.

Indeed Goliath's presence was intimidating. Israel had a choice. Israel could have either fought back or they could have shrunk back in fear. Just as Israel had a choice when Goliath confronted them—you also have a choice. You can either stand still in awe of Goliath—paralyzed by his splendor—or you can choose to cut off his head. Choose to defeat Goliath and cut off his head.

Fear will enslave you. Intimidation will keep you in bondage. Israel was being bullied. Goliath wanted to enslave an entire generation. Don't surrender to fear. Don't surrender to intimidation. Your obedience today can set generations free from the bondage of fear.

Your stagnation today will enslave future generations. Leaders choose to stand up for others in adversity. Kings choose to fight back in crisis. Don't shrink in fear. Let God lead your emotions. God is bigger than the giants that you face.

Day 9

MENTAL TENACITY: KINGS KILL PROBLEMS

Let's examine David's mental fortitude during this time of war. Notice what David declared in 1 Samuel 17:26 KJV, "And David spake to the men that stood by him, saying, What shall be done to the man that killeth this Philistine, and taketh away the reproach from Israel? for who is this uncircumcised Philistine, that he should defy the armies of the living God?"

Notice David's key words, "Who is this uncircumcised Philistine?" David, not only understood and recognized his Covenant with God—he also did not allow "the problem" to immobilize his authority. Kings kill problems and lead in times of chaos. Kings innovate and choose to find solutions in the midst of problems.

Although David was not the king—he held a king's mindset. Notice David's words, "Who is this uncircumcised Philistine?" Take note on how David addresses the problem. David never called Goliath by his name. In fact, David continued to call Goliath, "Uncircumcised Philistine." Take careful note of this kingly language that David decided to use.

Remember, the name "Goliath" means "Splendor." The men in Saul's army, including King Saul, used fear-based language, and their word selection revealed the fruit that was buried deep within the walls of their hearts. Your word selection and language reveals what's rooted deep within the borders of your heart.

The men in Saul's army, including King Saul, magnified Goliath. They magnified "Splendor" while David magnified God. David focused on God while Saul, and his army, focused on the strength and power of Goliath. The language of faith sounds different than the language of fear. Prioritize your focus. Change your language. Focus on Christ. Focus on the solution.

David's language was different. Throughout the entire chapter, every time David spoke, he referred to Goliath as the "Uncircumcised Philistine." David was not normal—he was not like the others. David was not like the rest of the army. In fact, David was not like his brothers. David was a king in development.

David's mental fortitude and mindset surpassed those around him. In fact, David had mentally killed this "Uncircumcised Philistine" long before he ever held a sword in his hand. David killed this "Uncircumcised Philistine" in his mind long before the battle ever materialized. David had already won the battle in his mind long before he was even given the opportunity to fight.

Remember, at this point, David was not yet a part of the king's army. David did not have a specific title or rank in Israel's army. He was not a captain, neither was David a part of the king's troop. David actions teach us that you don't need a title in order to lead. You don't need a specific rank to lead and to inspire others.

David led without a title. David led and influenced those who outranked him. Oftentimes, we let our title, or the lack thereof, limit our ability to lead. Many times we let our rank and position constrict us. Don't shrink. Let God use your gifts, talents, and abilities for His Glory.

Although rank, position, title, and authority all have their proper place—leadership and the autonomy to lead are not confined by a title. Leadership is a mindset. You don't need a title in order to lead. Look at Saul—he held the title as "King" and yet he did not lead Israel. Just because you have the title, your title alone does not make you a leader.

Just because you "look" the part, that does not make you a leader. Leadership is not defined by looks, status, stature, title, or position—leadership and leaders come in many forms.

Day 10

GOD LOOKS ON THE HEART

But the Lord said unto Samuel, Look not on his countenance, or on the height of his stature; because I have refused him: for the Lord seeth not as man seeth; for man looketh on the outward appearance, but the Lord looketh on the heart.

1 SAMUEL 16:7 KJV

When God raises up leaders, God looks on the heart. God taught Samuel this very key leadership principle in 1 Samuel 16:6-7 KJV, "And it came to pass, when they were come, that he looked on Eliab, and said, Surely the Lord's anointed is before him. But the Lord said unto Samuel, Look not on his countenance, or on the height of his stature; because I have refused him: for the Lord seeth not as man seeth; for man looketh on the outward appearance, but the Lord looketh on the heart."

God, who is the Ultimate Leader, looks at the heart. Samuel almost made the same mental mistake that many leaders make when they're building a team—they look on the outside. Most leaders are hidden. Many leaders are found in the field or in the backside of a desert.

Many leaders aren't dressed like kings. Most leaders don't "look" the part. Most leaders don't "look" like kings. In fact, most leaders are overlooked. Here's the point: you will find most leaders working in the field—hidden and tucked away.

1 Samuel 16:11–12 KJV teaches us this "hidden" leadership principle, "And Samuel said unto Jesse, Are here all thy children? And he said, There remaineth yet the youngest, and, behold, he keepeth the sheep. And Samuel said unto Jesse, Send and fetch him: for we will not sit down till he come hither. And he sent, and brought him in. Now he was ruddy, and withal of a beautiful countenance, and goodly to look to. And the Lord said, Arise, anoint him: for this is he."

These "unknown leaders" are in fact some of God's greatest weapons. These unknown leaders aren't necessarily in the spotlight but they've been hidden, training for years in the background. God has hidden you for a purpose. God has hidden you for such a time as this. Don't despise working in the field. Don't despise working in obscurity—your time will come.

David didn't allow the obscurity of his platform to harden his heart. While David was working in the wilderness—tending to his father's sheep—he was being used by God to sharpen his talent, skills, and abilities. While you're in the field, sharpen your skill set. While you're in the background, develop your gifts. While you're in the wilderness, take this time to develop and strengthen your relationship with God.

God prepared David in private before the public platform was presented. Let God develop your mental fortitude while you're in the background. Get stronger when you're behind the scenes. Get stronger when you're not in the public light. With titles come weight and responsibility.

Choose to lead when you're in the wilderness. Choose to lead when no one is watching. Learn to develop your mental muscle when you aren't leading others—then when it's your time to lead, you'll be ready to execute swiftly, accurately, and consistently.

There's a time to learn, and there's a time to execute. There's a time to lead, and there's a time to bow. There's a time to kill, and there's a time to retreat. David understood these principles well. David knew that it was time to kill. While Saul retreated—a new king was minted right before his eyes.

Fear will cause you to retreat. Fear will cause you to abandon your destiny. Fear will paralyze your forward momentum. Fear will chain you to the "Splendor" of the problem instead of tackling it head-on. Fear will cause you to shrink. Fear will enslave you to the mistakes of the past. Choose to be set free and move forward in your destiny.

In the Name of Jesus, I declare that you are set free from the paralytic grip of fear.

In the Name of Jesus, I declare that fear no longer has a hold on your mind.

In the Name of Jesus, I declare that fear has no place in the walls of your heart.

I declare, in the Name of Jesus, that fear has no power over your life, destiny, dreams, and future.

In the Name of Jesus, I declare that you, your house, and your mind is set free from the sting and paralytic venom of fear.

Let the Blood of Jesus govern your thoughts. Let the Blood of Jesus cover your mind.

Let the Blood of Jesus cover your heart. Let the Blood of Jesus lead and cover your actions.

In Jesus' Name. Amen.

Day 11

A KING IN SHEEP'S CLOTHING

Remember, Goliath's name means, "Splendor." In fact, his very presence was intimidating to many. However, David wasn't intimidated by this "Uncircumcised Philistine." David was not afraid of this intimidating problem. Saul retreated and David emerged. Saul shrank and David was enthroned. Saul tried to delegate away what God had told him to kill.

One way to identify a king who's disguised in sheep's clothing is to find out what they are willing to kill. Find out what they are not afraid of. Kings kill problems. Kings solve problems. Kings are anointed to tackle problems that normal people cannot solve.

Before David was king, he killed what Saul was afraid to kill. David killed what Saul was enslaved to. Fear enslaved the heart of Saul, and he bowed to the authority of fear.

God sets kings in place to bring peace. God sets kings in place to bring order. God sets kings in place to bring prosperity. God sets kings in authority to break generational cycles. God sets kings in authority to break generational chains and curses. God sets righteous kings in place to lead and cover nations.

God taught David while he was in obscurity. God raised up David when others overlooked him. David's heart remained pure even when others discounted him. A leader will not allow the opinions of others to contaminate their heart. You cannot exalt the opinion of man. Don't get bitter in the wilderness.

Remember, while everyone magnified "Goliath," David trusted in God and declared, "Who is this uncircumcised Philistine that defies the armies of the Living God?" Leaders tackle problems differently. Leaders kill threats differently. Leaders think about problems differently. Kings tackle problems differently. Leaders have a peculiar approach to handling and solving problems. Choose to lead and think differently.

Problems are the doorways to kingship, and those who solve them hold the keys that unlock their next level. David had the solution—kill Goliath.

Day 12

THE HEAD OF GOLIATH

Therefore David ran, and stood upon the Philistine, and took his sword, and drew it out of the sheath thereof, and slew him, and cut off his head therewith. And when the Philistines saw their champion was dead, they fled.

1 SAMUEL 17:51 KJV

Notice in 1 Samuel 17:51 KJV, David ran towards the problem. Leaders run towards problems. After David had used his slingshot to strike the head of the Philistine with a stone, he ran toward the problem and he completed the kill. Kings complete kills. Leaders finish the task and the assignment at hand.

After the Philistine was subdued, according to 1 Samuel 17:51 KJV, David ran up to the Philistine and stood over him. Notice, the Bible declares that David "stood over" the giant. One of the spiritual leadership lessons, in this moment, is that God always triumphs over the enemy. David's prophetic act signaled to the enemy that God triumphs over fear.

The fear that once paralyzed the nation was now permanently disabled. After David had used the slingshot to knock down Goliath, David could have let Goliath, "the problem", lie there, but notice what David did in 1 Samuel 17:51 KJV, "David ran, and stood upon the Philistine, and took his sword, and drew it out of the sheath thereof, and slew him, and cut off his head therewith."

David took the Philistine's sword, slew him, and severed the head of the giant for all to see that the Philistine's champion—was dead. Sometimes you have to cut off the head of the giant in order to make a statement to the enemy.

When David struck down Goliath with the sling and stone, the Philistine army remained. It was only when David ran up to the carcass and had cut off the head of their champion, that's when the Philistine army fled. When the Philistines saw the head in the hand of David, it was a clear and decisive victory.

Problems have clear and decisive solutions. Become the answer. Hold the solution in your hand and choose to slay giants. God is raising up "giant slayers." God is raising up "problem solvers." David's obedience did not only chase away the Philistines, but his actions inspired generations to function in their purpose. Your obedience inspires generations to obey God and to function in their call.

What has God called you to kill? What assignment are you called to complete? Your obedience today will unlock faith in others. You never know how much of an impact your actions can have on generations. Choose to obey Christ and kill fear.

After the kill, notice what 1 Samuel 17:52 KJV declares, "And the men of Israel and of Judah arose, and shouted, and pursued the Philistines, until thou come to the valley, and to the gates of Ekron. And the wounded of the Philistines fell down by the way to Shaaraim, even unto Gath, and unto Ekron."

Your obedience will give others the faith to pursue giants. Israel was once paralyzed by fear, and now, because of David's obedience, an entire army has the faith to pursue the enemy.

Your obedience will inspire generational armies to pursue, fight, and function in their call.

Notice what 1 Samuel 17:52 KJV declares, "And the men of Israel and of Judah arose." Look at this powerful principle nestled in this verse—Judah arose! When you kill the giant, you unlock hidden praise. This is the first time in this chapter that Judah was ever mentioned. Now that David has killed the thing that stunted Israel's faith—Judah arose.

Your actions will unlock generations who have shriveled back in fear and defeat. When you're governed by fear—your praise gets lost. Faith produces praise. Your obedience strengthens those who are weak and weary. Be the solution. Slay the giant. No matter the problem—become the solution and kill the giant.

Day 13

KINGS ARE BORN IN CRISIS

Kings are minted in times of crisis. The main responsibility of kings, especially during times of crisis, is to cultivate an environment of peace, comfort, safety, confidence, and clarity. Saul, delegated away what he was supposed to lead and control. The giant was Saul's responsibility.

Saul aided to the chaotic environment by giving in to fear. Saul retreated when he was supposed to war. When kings improperly retreat, those under their stewardship shrink. Don't shrink when God has given you the authority to be bold. It's time to war.

When kings retreat, the enemy has the opportunity to advance on the territory that God has promised you. Do not retreat. Choose to war. David knew this principle well. He knew when it was time to war and when it was time to retreat—kings discern the difference.

When Saul retreated, his actions opened the door to the enemy to occupy the ground that was meant for Israel to conquer. Although Saul wore the crown, David was anointed to function as king. Saul held the position, but David carried the mantle.

Just because someone wears the crown, it does not mean that they're graced for kingship. There are many kings who wear crowns, and they only serve as "placeholders." There are many kings who occupy thrones without authority. David was graced for kingship, but his time had not yet come.

Although David was graced for kingship, he did not worship the title. Although David was anointed to be king, he did not grow impatient. David served. David sharpened his skills in the wilderness. David honored God by understanding authority. Although David had the output and production of a king, David knew that God had set Saul as king. Kings understand authority. Kings understand God's timing. Kings understand protocol.

David understood that he was not the king. Just because David killed Goliath, this one act did not establish him as king. Don't allow your one act of victory to deceive you into thinking that you're ready for kingship. David knew that he was being prepared. David did not confuse his preparation for his future promotion. Your preparation has purpose. Kings are prepared. Kings are placed. Kings are positioned. Kings are groomed. Kings understand when it's their time to be enthroned.

Day 14

DON'T COVET THE CROWN

At the moment, the crown was on Saul's head. Although David was next in line, he did not covet the crown. Don't covet the crown. Don't covet the position. Don't covet the promise. Don't magnify the title. Don't worship the title. Don't turn the position into an idol. That's what Saul made the mistake of doing; he idolized the crown instead of honoring God. Saul magnified and idolized the voice of the people instead of magnifying and worshipping God.

Saul's heart had turned away from worshipping the True and Living God. Saul had turned to serve other idols. Although Saul did not worship the physical pagan false gods of the time, he worshipped something deeper. He worshipped the opinion of people.

Saul had a habit of misprioritizing his worship. Saul not only worshipped the opinion of man but he also battled an "Internal Goliath"—he bowed to fear. In fact, Goliath revealed what was already in Saul's heart. Goliath was the public manifestation of what Saul was worshipping privately. You cannot publicly kill what you secretly bow to privately. Fear was one of Saul's lords. Saul could not defeat Goliath because fear had already ruled his heart long before Goliath came on the scene.

In fact, there were other gods in operation as well—Saul worshipped the opinion of men. Kings consider counsel. Kings weigh counsel. Kings do not worship the opinion of man. Kings obey God. Redirect your worship and honor God through your actions in private and in public.

When it was time to publicly kill Goliath, Saul could not publicly kill something that he was struggling with privately. You cannot kill what you fear. In fact, when the threat came, Saul couldn't call upon his other gods to kill the threat.

Remember the decree that went out from Saul's throne in 1 Samuel 17:25 KJV, "And the men of Israel said, Have ye seen this man that is come up? surely to defy Israel is he come up: and it shall be, that the man who killeth him, the king will enrich him with great riches, and will give him his daughter, and make his father's house free in Israel." Saul tried to get his men to kill the threat. You can't delegate away what God has ordered you to kill. Even his men were afraid and could not muster up the courage to kill Goliath.

Remember, Saul, the head of Israel, worshipped fear. So everything under his authority bowed to the same god—the god of fear. The spirit of fear. Fear ruled the army. Fear ruled the kingdom. Fear ruled the head. When the head worships another god, the body loses authority, both spiritually and naturally. The same gods that Saul worshipped in times past could not save him in the time of trouble.

God crushes idols—there is no competition in Him. When kings serve other idols—although they wear the crown—they lose power, authority, influence, access, and honor. When David held the head of Goliath in his hand, this sent a signal to the army, and to the king, that a new authority was in operation both spiritually and naturally. The head of Goliath was a victory for David, but to Saul, Goliath's head was a constant reminder of the authority that he had lost and a reminder of what he should have killed.

Don't let fear paralyze your kill. Kill what God has told you to destroy. Kill pride. Kill fear and pursue what God has told you to pursue. Do what God has told you to do. God is raising up new kings who will not bow to fear. God is raising up new kings who will not worship fear. These new leaders aren't afraid of running toward Goliath and cutting off his head. These new leaders aren't afraid of leading through action.

These new leaders aren't afraid of leading through execution. These new leaders aren't afraid to kill what everyone else is running away from. God is raising up a new generation of leaders who will honor God and aren't afraid of tackling "Goliath-sized" problems. Choose to rise up. Arise and sever the head of Goliath.

———————— Day 15 ————————

AFTER THE KILL

And David took the head of the Philistine, and brought it to Jerusalem; but he put his armour in his tent.

1 SAMUEL 17:54 KJV

David brought the head of Goliath back home. After the kill, David's status rose. After the kill, David's influence soared. After the kill, David's authority shifted. After the kill, David's rank elevated in the spirit and in the natural. After the kill, David established the pattern for generations to follow.

After the problem was solved, promotion came. Although David was anointed as king, he was not recognized for killing lions and bears in the field. David received honor and authority for killing what kings could not kill. The lion and the bear are your "reasonable service." The lion and the bear were preparation for what was to come.

Kings are recognized by their kill. Kings are recognized by their accomplishments. Kings are recognized by what they've conquered. Kings are recognized by the battles and wars that they've won. David's time in the wilderness was critical to David's leadership development. If David had not killed the lion and the bear in private, then he would not have been prepared to kill the giant in public. Don't despise small private beginnings, they were designed to prepare you for kingship.

1 Samuel 17:54 KJV declares, "And David took the head of the Philistine, and brought it to Jerusalem; but he put his armour in his tent." This wasn't David's first kill. David had previously killed the lion and the bear and handled their carcasses—and now he wasn't afraid to handle the head and the carcass of this giant.

Notice what 1 Samuel 17:54 KJV declares, "And David took the head of the Philistine, and brought it to Jerusalem; but he put his armour in his tent." David held the bloody and gory head of Goliath in his hand and brought it back to Jerusalem. He also handled the carcass of Goliath. In order to remove Goliath's armor, he had to touch Goliath's bloody body.

Kings handle bloody matters. Kings handle what others deem gory. Kings handle complicated matters. David held the head of the threat in his hand while Saul watched on the sidelines. Don't watch on the sidelines. It's time to kill.

God is raising up kings who will choose to obey Him and to follow His Commandments. God is raising up leaders who aren't afraid of killing giants. God is raising up leaders who aren't afraid of tackling Goliath-sized problems while keeping their hands clean and their hearts pure. Choose to be the solution.

Be the solution in business. Be the solution in government. Be the solution in media. Choose to be the solution in the faith community. Choose to be the solution in your family. Choose to be the solution in education. Be the solution in creative arts. Whatever mountain(s) God has called you to conquer, choose to be the solution.

God is raising up new leaders in government who aren't afraid of tackling Goliath-sized problems. God is raising up leaders who aren't afraid to represent Him on Capitol Hill and in City Hall. God is raising up judges, congressmen, congresswomen, senators, mayors, governors, and presidents who will serve and honor Him. God is raising up leaders who will tackle Goliath-sized problems that others are running away from.

Don't retreat. Be the solution. God is raising up generals in business who are bold enough to lead and innovate for Him. God is raising up leaders in media who aren't afraid of tackling issues with honor and integrity.

God is raising up families who will choose to represent Christ in the face of adversity, conflict, and crisis. God is raising up leaders in education who aren't afraid of pouring into the next generation and teaching others how to lead in crisis. God is raising up new leaders in faith who are bold and will not compromise in the face of the enemy.

God is raising up new leaders in creative arts who will create for Him and stand for Him—both in public and in private. God is raising up leaders who will not bow to fear. God is raising up leaders who are not afraid to lead through tumultuous times. Don't let external obstacles derail you from pursuing your purpose. What's paralyzing you? Choose to divorce yourself from fear and move forward in purpose.

Day 16

A NATION GOVERNED BY FEAR

Fear gripped Israel. Fear stunted the forward momentum of Israel. What's stunting your momentum? Why are you afraid of taking the next step? Maybe, it's fear? Maybe, it's doubt? Maybe, it's uncertainty? Maybe, it's the weight and condemnation of past mistakes? Maybe, it's intimidation? No matter the case, no matter the circumstance, no matter what challenge comes your way—choose to trust God and know that He has your back.

God is the Author of your forward momentum. Choose to move forward in Christ. Choose to move forward in what He's called you to do. Don't let fear paralyze your momentum. Don't let Goliath stunt your progress. Don't let Goliath stunt your growth.

Goliath was sent to intimidate Israel. In fact, Goliath was sent to enslave Israel. Don't allow fear to enslave your purpose. You were called to win. You were called to fight back. You were called by God to slay Goliath and to set your family free from the bondage of fear. Don't bow to fear. It's time to strike. Don't retreat. It's time to execute on what God has given you to accomplish.

Goliath was sent as a distraction to interrupt your destiny. His intimidation tactics were sent as a distraction to derail your focus. Don't let Goliath derail your progress. Goliath was sent to cause you to retreat. Don't back down. Use the gifts, tools, strategies, strengths, and abilities that God has given you to win.

When it's time to strike, choose to remember the principles and lessons of the past. When David killed Goliath, he used a sling and stone to strike down Goliath, but when it was time to take off Goliath's head, he used a sword. Kings know when it's time to upgrade their weapon. Different times call for different weapons.

Like David, you may start off using the sling and the stone that you used in the field—but when it's time to kill something that you've never killed before, you have to use an unconventional weapon. Kings stay flexible. Kings innovate in times of turmoil.

According to 1 Samuel 17:51 KJV, David did not hesitate; he ran upon the Philistine and quickly took the sword out of Goliath sheath and slew the giant. "Therefore David ran, and stood upon the Philistine, and took his sword, and drew it out of the sheath thereof, and slew him, and cut off his head therewith. And when the Philistines saw their champion was dead, they fled." David innovated on the spot. David decided to strike in the moment. David used the weapons, skills, talents, and abilities that he knew to use in order to kill Goliath.

1 Samuel 17:50 KJV declares, "So David prevailed over the Philistine with a sling and with a stone, and smote the Philistine, and slew him; but there was no sword in the hand of David." David conquered the problem without the conventional weapon—the sword.

What's in your hand? What's at your disposal? What skills, talents, gifts, and abilities have you sharpened in the wilderness? Before you strike down Goliath, choose to sharpen the gifts that God has given you in the wilderness. You can either become bitter in the wilderness or you can choose to use the gifts, talents, skills, and abilities that God has given you. Sharpen the gifts while you're hidden.

Day 17

DON'T GROW BITTER

David was publicly anointed, by Samuel, to be king—and yet he continued to work in the field. David could have become bitter while he waited on the manifestation of the promised mantle. In fact, David could have complained while he looked over the sheep in the field. David's heart wasn't focused on man's opinion. David's heart wasn't distracted by the position or status that he "should have" had. David diligently developed his skills in the background until it was time to execute in the foreground. Public stages and platforms will crush those who aren't prepared. David's preparation in private equipped him to execute in public.

May your private victories serve as private preparation for your global stage. Your seemingly minor private victories are critical for your future success. David knew that it was time to release the weapons that God had been strengthening and sharpening in private.

It's time to release the weapons. It's time to release the gifts, talents, and abilities that God has been developing within you. David was prepared when he faced Goliath. David was ready to conquer the enemy in private and in public.

What are you keeping alive in private that God has told you to kill? What private fears has God told you to crush? What private insecurities has God told you to surrender to Him? What has God told you to kill, crush, and destroy in private?

Rejection cannot cling with you into the next season. Depression cannot go with you to the next level. Rejection cannot go with you into the next season. Anything that's not like God cannot go with you into the next season. Crush the habits that draw you away from His Presence.

Divorce yourself from "Heart Habits" that pull you away from the heart of God. James 4:8 KJV declares, "Draw nigh to God, and he will draw nigh to you. Cleanse your hands, ye sinners; and purify your hearts, ye double minded." God doesn't raise up double-minded kings. He raises up those with clean hands and a pure heart.

Day 18

DRAW NIGH TO GOD

Draw close to Christ in private. Draw close to Him in public. Draw close to Him in every season. Surrender your private actions to Him. Surrender your whole heart to Him. Let your life reflect the Heart of Christ in private and in public. Public platforms aren't built overnight. When God raises up kings, He prepares them in private. Your private preparation is critical.

Before David conquered Goliath, David consecrated himself in private. Before David put a sling in his hand, David knew God. David trusted God. Kings fall when they try to use their gifts, talents, and abilities apart from God. Saul tried to function as king in his own strength, power, might, and authority.

1 Samuel 13:13 KJV declares, "And Samuel said to Saul, Thou hast done foolishly: thou hast not kept the commandment of the Lord thy God, which he commanded thee: for now would the Lord have established thy kingdom upon Israel for ever." 1 Samuel 13:13 KJV declares that Saul did not follow God's instructions. As king, Saul was to submit and surrender to God's Way of doing things.

Saul thought that he could do things his way. Saul thought that he could overrule what God had instructed him to do. Kings follow God's instruction. Submit to God's Way of doing things. 1 Samuel 15:23 KJV declares, "For rebellion is as the sin of witchcraft, and stubbornness is as iniquity and idolatry. Because thou hast rejected the word of the Lord, he hath also rejected thee from being king." Rebellion perverts kings. Stubbornness crushes kingdoms. Saul rebelled against God, and his heart was stubborn.

When God gave Saul instructions to carry out, Saul thought that his way was more prudent than God's. Saul thought his way was more expedient. In fact, Saul's stubbornness was a manifestation of an internal god that he worshipped internally—you guessed it, he idolized fear. He magnified what people thought of him. Saul worshipped the thoughts and opinions of man more than he reverenced and honored God.

Fear will cause you to stray away from God's Voice. Fear will cause you to disobey God's Voice and Instruction. Fear will rent the kingdom from your hand. 1 Samuel 15:28 KJV declares, "And Samuel said unto him, The Lord hath rent the kingdom of Israel from thee this day, and hath given it to a neighbour of thine, that is better than thou." Saul bowed to fear. David bowed to and honored God. Kings choose to honor and trust God.

Day 19

CAN GOD TRUST YOU?

Can He trust you to lead His people? Can He trust you to listen and to follow His Instruction? Can God trust you to obey Him—both in private and in public? Can God trust you to obey Him even when it's inconvenient? Can God trust you to hear and to obey His Voice—even when the voices around you are rising?

In times of distress, whose voice is louder—God's or man's? In times of crisis, whose voice is louder—faith or fear? Whose voice do you magnify when it's time to kill Goliath—God's or man's?

Crush fear and kill Goliath. Crush doubt and kill Goliath. Crush anxiety and kill Goliath. Crush depression and kill Goliath. Crush doubt and kill Goliath. When you crush and kill the enemy that has been taunting your generational bloodline for years, you open the platform for others to flourish.

When David killed Goliath, he opened the door for Israel to flourish. When David killed Goliath, he broke the paralytic fear that chained Israel to its impotency. Fear will chain you to the failure and failed attempts of the past. What has you chained to the past?

It's time to look forward. It's time to look to the future. It's time to look past the enemy and move forward in what God has called you to do. Ignore what the enemy is trying to tell you. No matter the mountain, no matter the giant, no matter the circumstance, choose to conquer what God has called you to conquer.

Choose to set a new leadership blueprint for others to follow. Choose to establish a new generational legacy. Choose to obey Christ, trust His Way of doing things and crush the plan of the enemy.

Day 20

NO FEAR.
IT'S TIME TO PURSUE

There is no fear in Christ. There is no doubt in Him. Choose to move forward in Christ and do what He has called you to do. Choose to crush Goliath and pursue everything that God has set before you.

Generations are depending on your obedience. Families are depending on your faithfulness. Generational bloodlines are shifted and transformed when you choose to submit to God's Word. Cycles are broken when you choose to obey God.

Galatians 5:1 KJV declares, "Stand fast therefore in the liberty wherewith Christ hath made us free, and be not entangled again with the yoke of bondage." Yokes are broken when you surrender to Christ. Old frameworks and ideals are shattered when you choose to obey Christ. Choose to obey Christ and watch your life shift.

Let His Word break yokes. Let His Word break bondages. Let His Word break generational curses. Let His Word break generational cycles. Let His Word break generational habits.

David, who was next in line for kingship, chose not to follow after the "fear pattern" of Saul—the previous king. God is raising up "Davids" who are willing to crush "Goliaths" and pursue everything that God has for them and their family.

David chose not to follow the fear blueprint of Saul. David chose not to follow the perverted pattern of Saul. David chose not to follow the previous pattern of "man-worship." David chose to follow God. David chose to follow God's Word.

Choose to follow God's Voice. Goliath was only the beginning. Killing Goliath was David's starting point while it was Saul's ceiling. Fear will limit the realm of your kingship. Fear will limit the magnitude of your authority.

Authority is given to those who are willing to obey and trust God. Power is released to those who choose to surrender to God's Voice. Breakthrough is birthed through those who choose to pursue and follow after Christ. Choose to pursue God with all of your heart. Don't let Goliath or any other obstacle stop you from pursuing your purpose. Choose to obey God and kill Goliath.

When you bring back the head of Goliath, it is proof that the enemy cannot stop you. Bringing home the head of Goliath serves as proof that fear will not rule your generation. Conquer Goliath. Kill fear and take authority over every assignment that God has given you. It's time to pursue. Don't let Goliath become an excuse. Seek God and kill Goliath.

Day 21

DECLARATION OVER FEAR

Let God lead the work of your hands. Let everything that you put your hands to do thrive. Let God teach your hands to war and your fingers to fight. May you pursue and conquer everything that God has set before you.

Let God teach you how to crush what's been tormenting and taunting over your family's bloodline. May you become the example for generations to follow. May you crush every debilitating generational cycle that's attached to Goliath. May you bring back the head of Goliath and conquer new territories.

May you crush the paralytic grip of fear. May you forever sever the bands of poverty and every form of spiritual lack and emotional deficit from off of your family.

May you crush and break the power of fear, perversion, and intimidation. May you break every form of generational oppression, rebellion, and control.

In the Name of Jesus Christ, may you conquer and overcome every form of fear, defeat, rejection, addiction, depression, and mental instability from your family's bloodline.

May you conquer and defeat every "Goliath" that plagues your thoughts, dreams, and vision. May you conquer and defeat every obstacle that stands in your way. May you tread upon and disarm every weapon of the enemy.

May you conquer and defeat every "champion" and threat of the enemy. May you take back your health. May you take back your wealth. May you take back your strength. May you take back your courage. May you take back the sustenance that the enemy has stolen.

May you forever be set free from Goliath's generational paralytic grip. May the Blood of Jesus cover you, guide you, and lead you into your next season.

Go and conquer Goliath. Cut off his head and let his reign never have an impact on you or your family's generational bloodline ever again.

In Jesus' Mighty Name. Amen.

FOR MORE BOOKS VISIT
www.VanceKJackson.com

www.ingramcontent.com/pod-product-compliance
Lightning Source LLC
Chambersburg PA
CBHW030916080526
44589CB00010B/327